Terrorism

Alison Jamieson

RAINTREE
STECK-VAUGHN
PUBLISHERS
The Steck-Vaughn Company

Austin, Texas

Global Issues series
Genetic Engineering
Terrorism
UN—Peacekeeper?

Cover: A Tamil Tiger ready for action.

Title page: A hijacked plane blown up by Palestinian terrorists at Dawsons Field in Jordan, 1970.

Consultant:
Derek Heater, Fellow of the Politics Association and former Dean of the Faculty of Social and Cultural Studies, Brighton Polytechnic, East Sussex, England

The publishers would like to thank Sue Scarfe for her help in preparing this book for publication.

U.S. Copyright © 1995 Thomson Learning

U.K. Copyright © 1995 Wayland (Publishers) Ltd.

This edition published by Raintree Steck-Vaughn Publishers, an imprint of Steck-Vaughn Company

All rights reserved. No part of this book may be reproduced or utilized in any form or by any means, electronic or mechanical, including photocopying, recording, or by any information storage and retrieval system, without permission in writing from the Publisher. Inquiries should be addressed to: Copyright Permissions, Steck-Vaughn Company, P.O. Box 26015, Austin, TX 78755.

Library of Congress Cataloging-in-Publication Data
Jamieson, Alison.
Terrorism / Alison Jamieson.
    p.   cm.—(Global issues series)
Includes bibliographical references and index.
Summary: Presents a historical background of terrorism and describes examples, concentrating on the Middle East and Northern Ireland.
ISBN 0-8172-4862-5
1. Terrorism—Juvenile literature. [1. Terrorism.]
I. Title. II. Series.
HV6431.J33   1995
909.82—dc20   95-5485

Printed in Italy. Bound in the United States.
2 3 4 5 6 7 8 9 0 02 01 00 99 98

Picture Acknowledgments

Camera Press *contents page*, 6, 10, 11, 19, 23, 24, 26, 27, 28 (below), 33, 34, 36 (left), 38, 41, 42, 43, 46, 47, 48, 49, 50-51, 52, 54, 55; Impact *cover*, 4-5, 28-29 (top), 56, 58, 60; Topham 7, 8, 12, 13, 15, 18, 25, 36 (right), 40, 44, 59; TRIP 14; Wayland Picture Library *title page*, 16, 20-21, 30, 31, 35, 39.

Maps are by Peter Bull.

CONTENTS

What Is Terrorism?	4
History and Definitions	18
The Middle East	30
Northern Ireland	42
What Can Be Done about Terrorism?	54
Sources of Quotes	61
Glossary	61
Further Reading	62
Further Information	62
Index	63

WHAT IS TERRORISM?

Terrorism is a problem that plagues people all over the world. Terrorist acts, including bombing, kidnapping, and hijacking, are a form of political violence designed to pressure a government or political party to acquiesce to the terrorist group's demands. Although terrorism has been around for centuries, it has spread to an international level only since the 1960s, when terrorists realized that the media could be used to publicize their interests.

Political violence arises for different reasons: the people may feel deprived in some way, they may feel that they suffer from social injustices such as racial or religious discrimination, or they may not agree with the ruling government. Riots, violent protests, and demonstrations are forms of political violence that call attention to the grievances of the people, but these are not considered terrorist acts. Revolutions and counterrevolutions are not forms of terrorism, either, but acts of war. In order for a violent act to be considered terrorism, there must be actual or threatened use of violence against certain people or symbolic places in order to get a larger group to give in to a small, usually elitist, group.

The differences between these forms of political violence might at first seem clear, but when it comes to classifying particular acts of violence, people often disagree. For example, some people would classify the bombing of abortion clinics as terrorism; others would classify those acts as violent protests. The words *terrorism* and *terrorist* are used by people who do not like or do not approve of the actions taken by the violent group. If the group's aims are considered correct or justified, then they are not called terrorists but freedom fighters or protesters, and instead of terrorism, they are staging armed resistance. Because of these differences in viewpoints, a specific definition of terrorism has never been completely decided.

WHAT IS TERRORISM ?

The political system called Fascism ended with the defeat of Nazi Germany in 1945. But there are still fears that fascist ideas of intolerance and racial discrimination may return, as demonstrated by this large anti-Fascist rally that was held in London in 1993.

Terrorists entered the Iranian Embassy in London in 1980 and held all the occupants hostage. One of the hostages was killed before the Special Air Services regiment of the British army staged a spectacular raid on the building. They killed five out of the six terrorists and freed the remaining nineteen hostages.

There are some aspects of terrorism about which people do agree. Terrorism is a form of war, although it doesn't involve the army of one country fighting the army of another, or even a large faction taking up arms against its own country. For example, the Confederate Army declaring civil war on the Union in 1861 was an act of war, not of terrorism. Terrorism usually involves a small group of people deciding to wage war on a much larger group. Often the larger group is a government. However, terrorism is not "official" war, so there are no "rules of warfare." For example, terrorists may torture or kill their prisoners.

Unlike soldiers in an ordinary army, terrorists do not wear uniforms or carry weapons openly; they are secretive and do not tell people that they are part of a fighting group. Terrorism always involves violence or the threat to use violence. But the most important single thing to remember about terrorism is that it causes terror for the purpose of bringing about change that is beneficial to the group.

"Just cause"
It is important to remember a person's point of view when listening to that person about a particular act. In the United States, a democratic country, we generally agree that if people elsewhere are being unfairly treated, if their rights are not respected, if they do not live in a democratic country, if peaceful means of protest have failed, and if they are not allowed to practice the religion of their choice, then rebelling against this state of affairs

WHAT IS TERRORISM?

is not called "terrorism," even if these people use violence. It is thought that they have a "just cause."

On the other hand, if a country is democratic, if people can state their religious and political opinions freely, and if a peaceful means of protest exists but is not used, then these people are not justified in using violence. These people are called "terrorists."

The liberation of Paris in August 1944 after four years of German occupation. Members of the French Resistance were often very young, and many were female. Although the Resistance blew up railroad lines and bridges and killed soldiers the way modern terrorist organizations do, it was considered heroic to fight the Nazi occupation.

Even with these distinctions, there are still questions. Some people believe that even if the cause is just or good, using violence is still wrong. The following question arises: "Can the aim of the group be so good that all actions, however violent, are justified?" Another way of asking this is, "Does the end justify the means?" In an act of war, for example, it may be thought justified for a group to shoot at soldiers, but never for people to kill innocent passersby or children.

Some people may agree with what a terrorist group does, even though they themselves do not take part in violent actions. Such people, called sympathizers, may

WHAT IS TERRORISM?

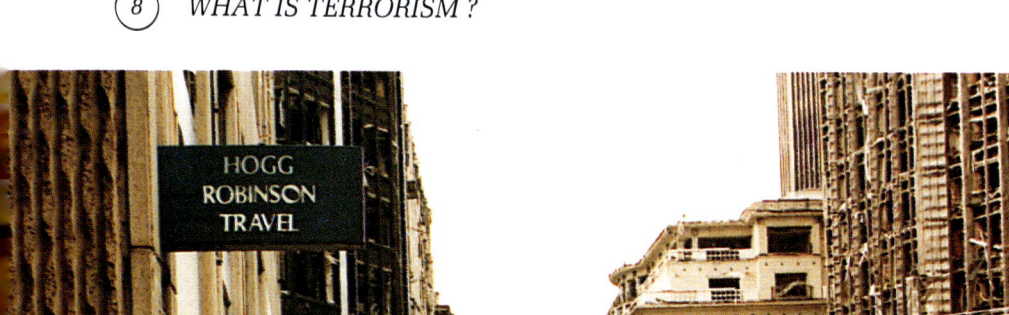

Cleaning up the rubble after the explosion of an IRA bomb in London, England, in April 1993.

give terrorists money or help terrorists avoid arrest by hiding them. The Chinese leader Mao Tse-tung called these supporters the "sea" in which the terrorist "fish" swim. When the fish have a deep sea in which to swim, it is hard to find them.

Other people may share the aim of a terrorist organization but disagree with the methods used to reach it. For example, almost all Arabs want to see an independent state of Palestine, but only a small number think that killing Israelis is the best way of going about it. Many people think Britain should stop ruling over Northern Ireland. They want the whole island of Ireland to be united into one single country. Even so, very few would agree that bombing British buildings or shooting British politicians is justified.

> ### ...
>
> **What people say about using violence**
> Here are a few things that terrorists, or people who support terrorism, say about using violence:
>
> "It takes the coming together of so many different elements for one person to go out and kill another…you can attribute a series of responsibilities or blame for things on to a whole category of people: things which are also concrete facts—the real unhappiness of people, deaths at the workplace, homeless earthquake victims, kids who die of heroin because someone allows it to happen; and also our own friends, companions killed during demonstrations, by the police…You have in your mind the model of society you want to construct—an idea of the right kind of relationships between people—mutual love, tolerance, help, and so on. You convince yourself that to reach this utopia [perfect state] it is necessary to pass through the destruction of the society which prevents your ideas from being realized. Violence is a necessary part of this destruction. If you accept the idea of violence you accept that it is a necessary price to pay, even though it has absolutely nothing to do with what will come afterwards." [1]
>
> "We want to continue to remind British people that their army continues to occupy part of Ireland and that the war will go on so long as they remain there." [2]
>
> "Every Communist must grasp the truth: 'Political power grows out of the barrel of a gun.'" [3]
>
> Here is what people who do not support terrorism say about terrorist violence:
>
> "Revolution, like war, is the strategy of the strong; terrorism is the strategy of the weak." [4]
>
> "Gangs of assassins must not be dignified with the word 'armies.' Terrorists should not be called 'freedom fighters.' Brutal murders must not be cloaked with that legal-sounding word 'execution.'" [5]

WHAT IS TERRORISM ?

Who are the terrorists?
Terrorists sometimes work alone, but usually they form groups to which they give a name, like the "Angry Brigades." The members of the group have at least two things in common: they share the same aims, and they agree that violence is necessary to achieve them. Terrorists believe in a cause. They think their cause is just, and they think it is worth fighting for. Sometimes they seem crazy or fanatical because they are ready to die for their cause. Just as they are ready to die, they are also ready to kill.

What is the difference between a terrorist and an ordinary criminal? Terrorists may commit the same crimes as ordinary criminals, but they do so for different reasons. Ordinary criminals think only about themselves; usually they want revenge, money, or recognition by the press. Terrorists act not for themselves, but for the group—they see themselves as champions for a cause.

What do terrorists do and how do they do it?
Ninety-five percent of all terrorist acts involve bombing, assassination, armed assault, hijacking, hostage taking, or kidnapping. Terrorists nearly always use weapons or explosives. Dynamite and other kinds of explosives are used to make bombs. Bombs are often hidden—for example, under a car or in a suitcase. Sometimes

Mao Tse-tung was a founding member of the Chinese Communist party in 1921. With the support of the Chinese peasants, who comprised 85 percent of the population, he brought about a revolution—which is considered an act of war, not of terrorism.

WHAT IS TERRORISM?

bombs are small enough to be placed inside an everyday object such as a radio. Bombs can be exploded by remote control or by using a timer device.

Sometimes bombs are not used to kill people, but to damage buildings. This is also terrorism, because it draws attention to the terrorists and their cause. Terrorists use guns of all kinds—from pistols and handguns to rifles and submachine guns. These can be used to kill or wound people or simply to frighten them. Using weapons to frighten people, not to hurt them, often happens during a hijacking, a kidnapping, or a hostage taking.

Two German hijackers take over a bus in Bremen, 1988. The two women in the foreground were taken hostage. The one on the left was later killed.

A hijacking is when terrorists take over a moving vehicle such as a plane, a boat, a train, or a bus. The driver may be threatened with a gun and terrorized into taking the vehicle to wherever the terrorists say. The people on the vehicle may be held hostage and used as bartering chips to be traded for money or the release of other members of the terrorist group from prison.

WHAT IS TERRORISM?

A firebomb was found hidden among clothing in a department store in Belfast, Northern Ireland, in 1994. Bombs are often made out of everyday objects so at a quick glance they will not arouse suspicion.

There are many terrorist groups in operation today. In Spain, the First of October Anti-Fascist Resistance Group (GRAPO) has been in operation since 1975. This group has been one of the most important "fighting communist organizations" (FCOs) in Western Europe. Another FCO, from Greece, called the Revolutionary Organization 17 November (17N), is a dangerous anti-American group that threatens U.S. interests in Greece. The Revolutionary Left, or Dev Sol, is another anti-American terrorist group, this one operating from Turkey. And the Red Army Faction, or RAF, from

WHAT IS TERRORISM? 13

Germany is Europe's longest surviving FCO. In 1991, the RAF attacked the U.S. Embassy in Bonn, Germany, with automatic weapons and assassinated a German government official who was working on transferring businesses from the state to private businesspeople.

This book focuses on some of the most prominent terrorist groups in operation today: the Irish Republican Army, or IRA, which is fighting for Northern Ireland's independence from Great Britain; the Palestine Liberation Organization, or PLO, an Islamic group fighting to regain lands from the Israelis; and the Islamic Brotherhood, which is fighting to purge the Middle East of Western influence.

These guns, discovered in an apartment in Belfast, were used by the Irish Republican Army (IRA). All terrorist groups use weapons—sometimes they steal them, while at other times they buy them illegally from other criminals.

14 WHAT IS TERRORISM ?

Eighty-four passengers and six crew members were on board this German Lufthansa plane when it was hijacked by Palestinian terrorists on its return from Majorca, Spain, in 1977. The captain was told to fly to Bahrain, then Dubai, and then finally to Mogadishu, Somalia. There, a joint German-British special forces team staged a dramatic rescue of the hostages.

WHAT IS TERRORISM? 15

The *Achille Lauro* hijacking

In 1985 an Italian cruise ship, the *Achille Lauro*, was hijacked in the Mediterranean Sea. There were four Palestinian terrorists on board with guns. For a few days they pretended to be ordinary passengers enjoying a cruise. Then they held the captain and crew at gunpoint. They forced all the passengers to gather in the ship's lounge and threatened to kill them. They told the captain to radio a message to shore explaining their demands. They wanted the Israeli government to release 50 Palestinians from prison.

Leon Klinghoffer enjoying a cruise aboard the *Achille Lauro* shortly before his brutal murder by Palestinian terrorists. The terrorists threatened to kill the passengers one by one every hour unless their demands were met.

The crew and passengers were held hostage for several days. One passenger in a wheelchair, Leon Klinghoffer—an American Jew—was shot dead and thrown overboard. There were only four terrorists against six hundred passengers and crew but the fear of being killed made everyone obey the orders. The hijackers said everyone

WHAT IS TERRORISM ?

was safe and agreed to leave the ship at Cairo in Egypt. The Egyptian government said it would fly them to another Arab country for trial. But the U.S. government was so angry when it learned about the murder that U.S. fighter planes forced the Egyptian plane carrying the hijackers to land in Italy. The hijackers were put on trial in Italy and given long prison sentences.

The difference between hostage taking and kidnapping is very simple. When the Palestinian terrorists hijacked the *Achille Lauro* it was no secret where they were. They were on a ship in the Mediterranean Sea. But

Captain John L. Testrake, the pilot of TWA Flight 847 hijacked in 1985, gave a television interview with a gun held to his head. He was forced to say that if anyone tried to launch a rescue operation all the passengers and crew would be "dead men."

WHAT IS TERRORISM?

when someone is kidnapped, he or she is taken to a secret place and no one except the kidnappers knows where it is. Kidnappers and hijackers do not usually want to kill anyone, even though they might do so. What they really want is to make a deal. They may free the hostages or the kidnap victim, but they always want something in exchange. Governments sometimes give in to terrorist demands. If they did not, the terrorists might kill the hostages.

Public opinion

During a hijack or kidnapping many people will follow the story on television and in the newspapers. There will be three different kinds of opinions. People may not approve of the terrorists, but think they should get what they want so that innocent people will not be killed. Or they may agree with the people who have done the hijack or kidnapping. They may think that the terrorists have a just cause, and that their demands should be met. Or people may say be very sad to think of innocent people being killed, but they believe terrorism is wrong. They may say, "No one should give in to terrorist demands under any circumstances. If anyone does, they will continue with terrorism."

Fact File

The South Molucca Story

The Molucca Islands are situated in the eastern part of the Indian Ocean. Once they were a Dutch colony; then, after World War II, they officially became part of Indonesia. The South Moluccan islanders wanted independence from the Indonesian government. There was some fighting, but the South Moluccans lost. Many left to live in the Netherlands. They thought the Dutch would help them win independence. But people either forgot about their wishes or ignored them. The South Moluccans formed a terrorist group in the Netherlands and carried out bombings and armed assaults. On two occasions they hijacked a train, killing some of their hostages.

In 1977 the Moluccan terrorists took five teachers and 125 children hostage in an elementary school. Some of the children were held for nineteen days before they were released. Then soldiers rushed into the school and captured the terrorists. The objectives of the group were to force the Dutch government to support their demands for independence; to attract public support for their cause; and to have their companions in prison released. The real target (the group of people whose attention the terrorists really wanted to attract) was the government of Indonesia.

HISTORY AND DEFINITIONS

The word "terrorism" came into use two centuries ago, during the French Revolution. It was used to describe a very violent period from 1793–94 known as the "Reign of Terror." This type of terrorism is used by a government against the population. It is known as state terrorism.

"Terrorism" appeared again in nineteenth-century Russia, to describe acts of violence against the rule of the czars. Those who carried out the violence were called revolutionaries and anarchists. They believed that the czars controlled all the power, wealth, and privileges in Russia, and that the ordinary people were oppressed—that is, they had no rights and no power. One group, the nihilists (from the Latin *nihil*, meaning "nothing"), wanted to sweep away the past altogether and create a new society based on reason and science.

The trial for the assassination of Czar Alexander II. There were several kinds of revolutionary violence in nineteenth-century Russia. Czar Alexander II was assassinated by nihilists in 1881.

HISTORY AND DEFINITIONS

Revolutionaries and anarchists had something in common with modern-day terrorists: they felt that violence was both necessary and honorable. They believed their cause was noble and just. People who are willing to die for a cause often say they are not afraid of death. They are ready to be martyrs—to die for what they believe in. They think their deaths will serve a good cause. They may even believe that using violence against the enemy cleans or purifies them.

Revolutionary and terrorist groups say they want freedom. The National Liberation Front in Algeria fought for freedom from French rule. Its members believed, and many people agreed, that France had no right to rule Algeria, and they resorted to terrorist acts targeting the French government. Other terrorist groups, such as the PLO or IRA, fight so that a particular race or religious group will be free to live in a particular place. This type of terrorism is called nationalist or religious terrorism.

But there is another kind of freedom terrorists fight for—freedom from class domination. Class domination is where one social class, usually made up of the very rich, has

Algerian rebels standing guard in front of a barricade, around 1958. The sign says "French Zone," a challenge to the French troops to enter if they dare.

20 HISTORY AND DEFINITIONS

power over the working class, the poorer section of the population. In South America, terrorist groups were formed in the 1960s in the hope that the poorest sections of the population would seize power from the rich people. They were inspired by the Russian anarchists and revolutionaries of the late nineteenth century, and became known as left-wing terrorists.

The hijackers of TWA Flight 847 forced the pilot to fly back and forth between Beirut and Algiers. In Beirut, 37 U.S. hostages were taken off the plane and hidden in the suburbs of the city for nearly two weeks.

Media Watch

The media and terrorism

Terrorist groups seek world attention. Some people think the media (television, radio, and newspapers) actually encourage terrorism. They say the media give "oxygen" to the terrorist group.

In 1985 two Lebanese terrorists hijacked TWA Flight 847, flying between Athens and Rome, and ordered the pilot to fly to Beirut, Lebanon. While the plane was at Beirut airport, American TV journalists filmed interviews with the terrorists and their hostages. They paid the terrorists a lot of money for this—some say about one million dollars.

Many people question whether the media should be allowed to do this sort of thing. But in the United States and most other democratic countries, freedom of the press prevents the passage of laws censoring this kind of news coverage or stopping criminals from being paid for interviews about their illegal activities.

HISTORY AND DEFINITIONS

Fact File

Franz Fanon and the National Liberation Front

Franz Fanon was an African doctor born in the French colony of Martinique. He went to work in a hospital in Algeria in the 1950s. At that time Algeria was under French rule, but a group called the National Liberation Front (FLN) was formed to fight for Algerian independence from the French. Fanon supported this group and thought their cause was a noble one. He wrote, "Violence is a cleansing force. It frees the native from his inferiority complex and from his despair and inaction; it makes him fearless and restores his self respect." [6]

The fighting in Algeria between the FLN and French government troops lasted from 1954 to 1962. Terrorism was used by both sides. The world was shocked to hear that French soldiers were torturing and murdering Algerian rebels in cold blood. It was also very costly for the French to fight the war there. In 1962, with the approval of the French people, Algeria was given full independence. In exchange, the rights of the French people living in Algeria were protected.

Left-wing terrorism

The South American left-wing terrorist groups called themselves guerrillas (soldiers). The best-known guerrilla was Che Guevara. He was killed in Bolivia in 1967.

In the 1960s there was a left-wing group in Uruguay called the Tupamaros. They wanted to win power for the peasants and workers. For several years the Tupamaros did not kill anyone. They had a Robin Hood image and many people would not even have called them terrorists. But by 1970 they had become more violent. They began to kill policemen and kidnap victims. Altogether they kidnapped 21 people—usually foreign diplomats or businessmen. One rich businessman was kidnapped and released only after $300,000 was paid to textile workers whose factories had been closed down.

On another occasion, 40 Tupamaros took over a whole town. No one paid much attention to them because they looked as if they were taking part in a funeral procession. They were all dressed in black and following a hearse. When they arrived in the town center they robbed three banks and took over the police station. They left the town after a shoot-out with the police.

The government became very tough with the Tupamaros and introduced special "war powers." People had become frightened of the Tupamaros, so they accepted a more severe kind of government. Very quickly the Tupamaros were defeated. In 1973 military forces took over power in Uruguay, and democracy was overthrown. In a way, the terrorists helped to destroy democracy—the opposite of what they had set out to do.

Left-wing terrorism began in the United States and in Western Europe in the late 1960s. The

Argentinian-born revolutionary Ernesto "Che" Guevara in 1960. He helped Fidel Castro bring about a revolution in Cuba. He established a guerrilla base in Bolivia in 1966, but was captured and shot by the Bolivian army in 1967. Che became a model for revolutionary groups in both Europe and North America.

HISTORY AND DEFINITIONS

Young guerrillas training for jungle warfare in Peru, 1993. They are members of Shining Path, a group that follows the teachings of Chinese leader Mao Tse-tung. Mao and Che Guevara both believed that revolutions should start in rural areas and then move to the cities.

Russian revolutionaries and the South American guerrillas were the heroes for these terrorist groups. In the United States the most famous organizations were the Symbionese Liberation Army, the Weather Underground, and the Black Panthers. The people who joined these groups were especially angry about Americans being sent to fight in Vietnam. They also felt that the U.S. government discriminated against blacks.

HISTORY AND DEFINITIONS

Media Watch

The Red Brigades

The Red Brigades were an Italian terrorist group that had kidnapped and murdered former Italian prime minister Aldo Moro in 1978. In 1980 they kidnapped a judge in Rome. The Red Brigades said they would free the judge on one condition: if messages written by the prisoners were printed in all the most important newspapers and read out on television. Otherwise they would kill him. Some of the newspapers printed the messages, even though they contained threats that the Red Brigades would kill more people.

The judge's 14-year-old daughter went on television. She read out one message that said her father was a pig and deserved to die. She did not really believe this, but she wanted to help free her father. Other newspapers refused to print the messages. They said the messages were "written by assassins whose hands are dripping with blood." The terrorists were pleased because they received so much attention. They freed the judge.

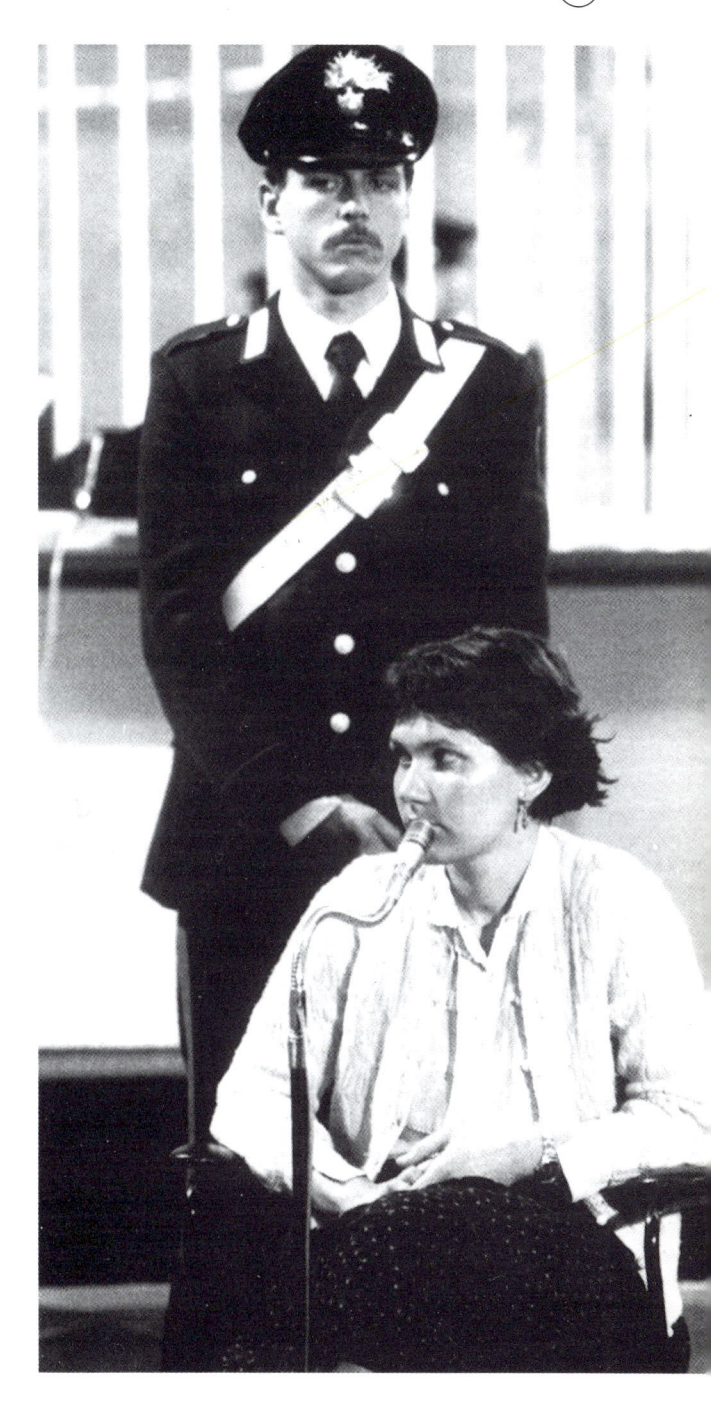

Italian Red Brigades terrorist Emilia Libera gives evidence in an Italian court, 1982. Libera was one of a group who kidnapped a U.S. NATO forces general in Verona, Italy, in 1981. Italian terrorists who confessed and gave information leading to the arrest of others were given shortened prison sentences.

In Europe the most influential groups were the Red Army Faction in Germany and the Red Brigades in Italy. They felt the working classes in their countries were being treated badly by their governments. They wanted to bring about a revolution and hoped the workers would take over power. They tried to attract attention and support for their cause by kidnapping, wounding, and killing important politicians, judges, and businessmen. They tried to make the working classes think that the politicians and big businessmen were evil and corrupt people. They thought the workers would then follow them and bring about a revolution.

All of these groups caused terror, but none of them was able to bring about a revolution. They did not succeed because the United States, Italy, and Germany were strong democracies, and a very small number of people believed that violence was the only way to change political situations.

Right-wing terrorism
Right-wing terrorism is very different from left-wing terrorism. Left-wing terrorists want power to be in the hands of the working classes (sometimes called the proletariat), with ordinary citizens in charge. The targets of left-wing terrorism are important people who are representatives, or symbols, of what the terrorists hate.

Right-wing terrorists think power should be very tightly controlled by a small number of people. People who disagree with the ruling group would be killed or sent away. Some right-wing terrorists believe that only their own race is pure and that all others are dirty or impure. They feel justified in doing anything to get rid of the impure people.

There is an association in the United States called the Christian Identity Movement. Its members believe in the supremacy or superiority of white people. They believe that Jesus Christ was not a Jew but a member of the Aryan race. They hate all Jews and non-whites and think that Jews have far too much power.

HISTORY AND DEFINITIONS

In 1987, 14 members of this group were put on trial and given long prison sentences. They had been planning to kill thousands of people by poisoning the water supply of two American cities. They wanted to terrorize the government and bring about its collapse. Then they hoped that another world war would break out—perhaps even a nuclear war. Their goal is the absolute triumph of the Aryan race, with the impure races being wiped out altogether. They think God will help them bring this about.

Hatred of a particular race, or of foreigners in general, has also led to terrorism in Europe. Turkish or North African people living in Germany have been attacked—sometimes killed—and their houses have been burned down. But some of the worst cases of racial or ethnic "cleansing" in Europe have taken place in Bosnia, former Yugoslavia. There, Serbian soldiers have tried to exterminate as many Muslims as possible by forcing them to flee or by killing them.

Right-wing terrorist groups have their heroes, too. Often they take Adolf Hitler as their role model. Hitler thought Jews were impure, and he had six million killed in extermination camps during World War II. He believed the only pure race was the Aryan race, which he called the master race.

(Below) German Führer Adolf Hitler addressing a rally. Hitler came to power in 1933. He wanted Germany to be the most powerful nation in Europe. His plan to kill all Jewish people was called The Final Solution.

(Below) Muslim and Croatian prisoners of war in Bosnia, former Yugoslavia, in 1993.

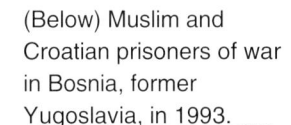

HISTORY AND DEFINITIONS

State terrorism
This brings us back to terrorism carried out by states or governments. Adolf Hitler was Führer, or leader, of Germany from 1933 until 1945. During that time he used terror and violence against German citizens, especially those of Jewish origin.

When a government openly inflicts acts of terrorism on its citizens, this is sometimes qualified as "terror," as in the French Reign of Terror, but not as terrorism. State-supported terrorism happens when a government helps a terrorist group by giving money or protection because it agrees with the group's aims.

Governments sometimes want to terrorize their enemies but they do not want do it openly. So they might pay a terrorist group to do some killing or bombing for them. This can have two advantages: first, it is cheaper than fighting an all-out war; second, the sponsor state doesn't need to admit to the terrorist act.

Many governments have sponsored or supported terrorism at different times. Libya is the country most often accused of this and is thought to have helped 30 terrorist groups at different times. The Irish Republican Army—discussed on pages 42–53—received one ton of deadly explosives and hundreds of rifles from Libya. The Libyan leader Colonel Mu'ammar Muhammad al-Gadhafi has admitted this, and says he was proud to help the IRA because it was fighting a war of independence from Great Britain.

Libyan leader Colonel Mu'ammar al-Gadhafi. Under his rule Libya has supported and sponsored terrorist acts in different parts of the world.

Libyan state terrorism led to an American act of war in revenge. In 1986 U.S. forces bombed the Libyan town of Tripoli. Hundreds of people were killed, including Colonel Gadhafi's adopted daughter.

Great Britain and the United States think that Libya was responsible for the bomb that exploded inside aircraft Pan Am Flight 103, which crashed over Lockerbie, Scotland, just before Christmas in 1988. It killed all 259 passengers and crew and 11 people on the ground. If Libya was responsible, then it might have been an act of retaliation against the United States for bombing Tripoli.

Even democratic countries sometimes support terrorism against countries or groups that they do not like. The United States gave money and arms to a rebel group in Nicaragua called the Contras in the 1980s. The Contras were fighting the democratically elected government of Nicaragua. The American government believed that helping the Contras was justified because the Nicaraguan government was sympathetic to communism. Also, because Nicaragua is geographically close to the United States, the U. S. government felt this was a threat.

Police standing by the wreckage of Pan Am Flight 103. The bomb that destroyed it was hidden in a suitcase. Investigators think it was originally loaded at Malta airport and then transferred to the Pan Am flight in Frankfurt, Germany.

THE MIDDLE EAST

Leila and Bana are Palestinian sisters aged eight and fourteen. They live in Nablus, a town on the West Bank. The area is so called because it lies to the west of the Jordan River. The West Bank, the Gaza Strip, and the Golan Heights are parts of the land formerly called Palestine. From 1920 until 1947, Palestine was ruled by Great Britain under an international agreement, or mandate. In the 1930s and 1940s there was a lot of fighting between Zionists (those who wanted to establish a separate Jewish state) and Arabs in Palestine, because each side felt it had a right to the land. British targets were also attacked because they were seen as the enemy occupier. In 1946, a Zionist terrorist group planted a bomb in the King David Hotel in Jerusalem, where the British headquarters was located. The bomb killed 91 people. After that the British left Palestine altogether.

An Arab demonstration in Gaza in 1957. Israel had tried to oppose Egypt's taking full control over the Suez Canal. Demonstrators are carrying an effigy of Israeli leader David Ben Gurion.

THE MIDDLE EAST

The United Nations (UN) decided that Palestine should be divided into two parts—Israel for the Jews and Palestine for the Arabs. The State of Israel was created in 1948. There was special sympathy for the Jews at that time because so many had been murdered by the Nazis during World War II. The Jews felt they needed to create a strong country—one that would be safe from any future attack. They began to extend their settlements outside the area decided by the UN. There were military battles on the borders of the Arab zones, and the Israelis won each time. In 1967 there was a war that lasted six days. It ended with the Israeli occupation of the Gaza Strip, the West Bank, East Jerusalem, and the Golan Heights.

In 1948 and again in 1967, many Arabs were obliged to leave their homes and jobs. Some went to live in refugee camps, where sometimes there was no water or electricity.

The Intifada

In 1987 Leila and Bana's parents, together with many other Palestinians, began to organize a protest against the Israeli occupation. It was a violent protest, but it did not aim to kill people. It was called the Intifada, or popular uprising. Sticks and stones were thrown at Israeli soldiers. Children took part in the Intifada, too—even very young ones. They were known as the *Shebab* (youth) army. There was some rivalry between the boys and the girls of the Shebab.

Wreckage of the Jewish quarter in Cairo, Egypt, in 1948, after explosions in which 25 people died. As many as 800,000 Palestinians had been forced to leave their homeland in 1948. This attack was proof of the anger and hatred many Arabs felt for the Jewish people at that time.

A map of the Middle East

Bana said, "There is a boy I know who is too frightened to join the demonstrations. I tell him, it is your duty to throw a stone and to become a martyr. It is your national duty. Girls in the strike forces [stone throwers] are just as good as the boys because we can run as fast as they can and throw stones as well. Soldiers are also stupid—they think it is more important to catch the boys, so we carry the flags and distribute the Intifada leaflets." [7]

Naturally the Israeli soldiers became angry when attacked and sometimes hit the stone throwers with their batons or shot at them. Over nine hundred Palestinians were killed in the Intifada, many of them children. Some Israelis were killed, too.

THE MIDDLE EAST 33

The Palestine Liberation Organization (PLO)

Yasser Arafat is chairman of the Palestine Liberation Organization (PLO). The PLO was founded in 1964 to fight for a homeland for the Palestinians. The PLO saw Israel as its enemy; it believed any methods were justified to destroy Israel in order to win a Palestinian state.

The PLO created terrorist groups. Their purpose was to carry out attacks against Israel and against countries friendly to Israel. In 1970 Palestinian terrorists hijacked three aircraft—an American, a Swiss, and a British one—and made the pilots land on an unused airfield in Jordan called Dawsons Field. There were 475 hostages. The hijackers called for the release of

Young Palestinians attacking Israeli soldiers on the West Bank, 1988. A whole generation has grown up here amid hatred and violence.

Palestinians from European prisons. Seven prisoners were freed; then the hostages were released and all three planes were blown up on the runway.

Black September
King Hussein of Jordan did not like the PLO carrying out terrorist attacks in his country, so in September 1970 he sent his army to attack their camps. Many were killed. Afterwards, a terrorist group called Black September was formed to take revenge for these killings and to continue the fight for Palestinian independence.

During the Olympic Games in Munich in 1972, eight Black September terrorists climbed over the fence of the Olympic village. The terrorists went to the building where the Israeli athletes lived, killed one, and took nine hostage. They said they would kill the hostages unless two hundred Palestinians held in Israeli prisons were freed. The Israelis refused to make a deal. The Germans set a trap: they said the terrorists could fly to Egypt if they let the hostages go. At the airport the trap

The Olympic village, Munich, Germany, during the hostage crisis. Eight terrorists climbing over the fence in the early hours of the morning were mistaken for late-night revelers returning home.

failed. German police opened fire on the terrorists. In the gun battle that followed all the Israeli hostages were killed, as were five of the Palestinians and a German policeman.

The Abu Nidal Organization (ANO)
From 1974, Yasser Arafat decided that "international" terrorism (involving citizens of other countries) was not helping his cause. He promised that from then on, the PLO would only attack Israeli military targets in Israel or in the Israeli Occupied Territories. Not all the members of the PLO agreed with Arafat. Some, like Abu Nidal, disagreed with, or rejected, what Arafat said. They formed the "Rejection Front." The Rejection Front terrorist groups said they would attack any Israelis, whether military or civilian, and also the citizens of any countries friendly to Israel, such as the United States and Great Britain. They also tried to kill "moderate" Arabs like Arafat, whom they considered traitors.

The Abu Nidal Organization is believed to have killed more than a thousand people in 20 countries since 1974. It was responsible for shooting the Israeli ambassador to Great Britain in London in 1982. It also carried out two attacks at the same time on December 28, 1985, at Rome and Vienna airports, when ANO members opened fire at the check-in desks for El Al, Israel's national airline. Altogether, 20 were killed, including four of the terrorists, who were shot by airport police.

The Israeli government was very angry after the shooting of its ambassador to Great Britain. It blamed the PLO, which at that time had its headquarters in Lebanon. A few days after the London shooting, Israeli armies invaded Lebanon and bombed Palestinian camps around Beirut. A civil war was going on in Lebanon at that time, and there were no forces to keep

Ain al-Hilweh, a Palestinian refugee camp in Lebanon, after it was bombed by the Israeli army in 1982.

THE MIDDLE EAST

law and order; nor was there a true government. A quarter of a million people had their homes destroyed, and two thousand were killed during the invasion. There was a terrible massacre in two refugee camps, Sabra and Shatila. The Israelis tried to justify this by saying that Palestinian terrorists were hiding there.

A peace agreement

Yasser Arafat continued his independence struggle from Tunis. In 1988 the PLO was invited to take part in a special meeting of the UN Security Council in Geneva. Arafat made a speech in which he said for the first time that the PLO accepted Israel's right to exist. He said the Palestinians would agree to peace with Israel if Israel would agree to leave the land it had occupied in 1967. The UN had already asked Israel to leave those territories.

(Below) Yasser Arafat, chairman of the Palestine Liberation Organization, together with Hanan Ashrawi, leader of the Palestinian delegation, in the peace talks with Israel.

(Above right) Israeli Prime Minister Yitzhak Rabin signs a letter to Yasser Arafat in which he accepts that the PLO is the rightful representative of the Palestinian people.

Israel could not accept the idea of a completely independent Palestinian homeland, but the government was willing to talk about peace. Finally in 1993 a peace plan was signed in Washington by Yasser Arafat and Israel's Prime Minister Yitzhak Rabin. The peace plan said that Israel would start to take away its soldiers from Jericho and the Gaza Strip and that the Palestinians could have their own police force there. It also said the Palestinians could begin to govern themselves after elections in 1994, but it did not give them complete independence.

Not everyone was happy about the peace agreement. Some Israelis thought the PLO still wanted to destroy Israel. And some Palestinians were angry because the agreement did not give them complete independence. Extremists on both sides decided to use terrorism, hoping to destroy the trust that had grown up between the PLO and the Israeli government.

Islamic fundamentalism

Nationalist terrorism has often been used in the Arab-Israeli conflict. But the conflict is not just about a homeland, it is also about religion.

Most of the religious terrorism in the Middle East has been carried out by followers of Islamic fundamentalism. Islamic fundamentalists believe that the law of Islam—the *Shari'a*—is a perfect, or divine law. This law was written hundreds of years ago and is contained in the Islamic bible, or Koran. The fundamentalists hate Israel because it occupies land that they say is holy Islamic territory, and they hate all Western countries that support Israel. They believe the United States is an imperial power in the Middle East and they do not like this because they consider Westerners to be immoral. They blame American "imperialism" when Arab countries, like Egypt, which are friendly to the United States, do not compel people to observe the laws of the *Shari'a*. Islamic fundamentalists want to cleanse, or purify, the Middle Eastern countries of Western influence and help them return to the religious purity of Islam.

Of course, very few Muslims are terrorists. But the most extreme fundamentalists believe they are justified in killing people who are against their ideas or whom they consider to be evil. They also believe that by dying for the cause of their *jihad* (holy war), they will go to heaven. Israel and the United States are particular enemies for Islamic extremists, who call America the "Great Satan."

Fact File

Kach
Baruch Goldstein lived near Hebron, on the West Bank. He was a member of an organization called *Kach*. *Kach* members did not want the Palestinians to govern themselves. They were afraid that if the Palestinians had any power, they would drive the Israelis out of their homes. In February 1994, Goldstein took a gun and killed 29 Palestinians while they were praying in a mosque in Hebron. He was killed in the riot that followed.

A Palestinian group called *Hamas* promised to take revenge for the deaths. In the space of one week *Hamas* terrorists planted one bomb on a bus and another one in a marketplace. They said they would continue to attack Israelis. They wanted independence for Palestine.

Ayatollah Khomeini (center) led an Islamic revolution in 1979 that forced the then ruler of Iran, the Shah, to go into exile. Later that year Iranian students stormed the American Embassy in Tehran, the capital of Iran, and held 52 U.S. citizens hostage for 444 days.

There are two main divisions in the Islamic faith; they are called Shi'a and Sunni. The Ayatollah Khomeini was an important leader of Shi'a fundamentalism. He and his religious followers brought about a revolution in Iran in 1979 and created an Islamic fundamentalist state. Iran has supported Shi'ite groups throughout the Middle East because it would like to get rid of all Western influences there and create a huge Islamic state.

Hezbollah

Iran has also sponsored a Shi'ite group in Lebanon called Hezbollah, meaning "party of God." Between 1982 and 1989, Shi'ite terrorists were responsible for 247 terrorist incidents and 1,057 deaths.[8]

Hezbollah carried out several terrorist attacks against the multinational peacekeeping force that had been sent to Lebanon to try to restore order. The worst of these took place in 1983. In April, a Hezbollah member drove a truck full of explosives at the wall of the U.S. Embassy, killing 63 people as well as himself. In October there was a similar attack against both the

French and American military headquarters. On that occasion, 241 American marines and 59 French soldiers died. This was the worst terrorist attack the world had ever seen, and with it, Hezbollah succeeded in one of its aims—the multinational peacekeeping force left Lebanon soon after.

But Hezbollah terrorism did not end there. Between 1984 and 1992, the group kidnapped around 30 Western journalists, professors, and businessmen. They were held, sometimes for years, in small dark prisons where they were chained up and could hardly move. A few fell ill and died. Hezbollah hoped to exchange them for large numbers of Shi'ite prisoners held by Israel. They also wanted money. In some cases money or arms were offered for the hostages' release. The Israelis also kidnapped two Hezbollah leaders in the hope of having some Israelis who were in prison in Lebanon freed.

The Islamic Brotherhood

Islamic fundamentalism exists in many other countries, including Pakistan, Afghanistan, India, Sudan, Algeria, and Egypt. The Egyptian Islamic Brotherhood, or Gama'a Islamiya, was formed in 1928. It started as a youth club, but by 1949 it had grown into a political movement of half a million members. One of the leaders of this group was named Sheikh Omar Abdul Rahman.

U.S. President Jimmy Carter (center) with Egyptian President Anwar Sadat (left) and Israeli Prime Minister Menachem Begin (right) shake hands on peace in 1979. President Sadat was murdered by Islamic fundamentalists on account of this agreement.

Muslim women wearing the traditional chador, a garment that covers the head, shoulders, and part of the face. Strict Muslims insist that all women wear this as a sign of modesty. They do not approve of the way Western women dress.

Tourism in Egypt (right) has dropped dramatically since the Islamic fundamentalists threatened to kill Western tourists. The Egyptian government says it lost $900 million in the first nine months of 1993.

During the 1970s he was a professor of religion in the town of Asyut, on the Nile River.

In 1979, a peace agreement was signed between Israel and Egypt. The Islamic fundamentalists did not approve of this. The Islamic Brotherhood decided to punish the Egyptian president, Anwar Sadat, for "betraying" Egypt and making peace with Israel. President Sadat was murdered in 1981. Sheikh Rahman is thought to have given the religious blessing for this murder. He was arrested, but there was no proof that he was guilty.

THE MIDDLE EAST

When he came out of prison, Sheikh Rahman went to the United States and began to preach in a mosque in Jersey City, New Jersey. Worshippers at this mosque were found guilty of the bomb attack on the World Trade Center in New York City in February 1993.

The Islamic Brotherhood thinks Egypt is too friendly with Western countries and is not a "true" Islamic state because Egyptians are not forced to follow Islamic law. They also hate Western tourists, who offend Islamic law by drinking alcohol and dressing improperly—especially women, with their makeup, short skirts, and low-cut dresses.

From January 1993 on, the Islamic Brotherhood officially warned Western tourists not to visit Egypt. Tourist buses and Nile river boats have been shot at, and some Westerners have been killed or injured. After that, there were fewer visitors to the tomb of Tutankhamen, the Sphinx, and the Pyramids. There were many attacks against Egyptians, too. The Egyptian authorities acted very cruelly against Islamic terrorists in the attempt to bring the attacks to an end.

Media Watch

Attack on the World Trade Center

The World Trade Center, with its twin towers (1,377 feet high), is the second tallest structure in the world. As of February 26, 1993, 80,000 people worked there and 50,000 visitors each day admired the view from the 110th floor.

On that fateful day Islamic fundamentalists exploded a bomb in an underground garage. The explosion, together with the smoke and poisonous fumes that spread throughout the building, killed six people and injured more than a thousand. A schoolteacher was stuck in an elevator in the dark for five hours with seventeen children. They did not panic, but sang songs and prayed.

Television journalists spoke to some of those trapped in the building and relayed messages from emergency crews. The situation was handled admirably—it was the first terrorist attack on American soil—but the bomb had given Americans a terrible shock.

NORTHERN IRELAND

Sean is 12, the youngest in a Catholic family of six children. He lives on Falls Road in Belfast, Northern Ireland. Sean is not surprised to see armored tanks on the streets and soldiers patrolling with machine guns—it is a common sight in Belfast, one he has grown up with. The games he and his friends play are a mixture of fun and danger. One of the most exciting is throwing stones at British soldiers and then running away. Sean is somewhat confused, because at school everyone says they hate all "Prods" and "Brits"—Protestants and British people. But Sean has started going to a youth club after school where he plays table tennis. The club is run by Father O'Doyle, a Catholic priest, who encourages Protestant children as well as Catholics to go there. Sean has discovered Protestant children love soccer and cars, just like he does, and they watch the same TV shows. In fact, they are not really that different from him after all.

Fergus is 13 and another avid table tennis player. He goes to the same youth club as Sean. His family is

Boys learned at an early age to throw stones at the soldiers in Northern Ireland. By their midteens, many were handling guns and rifles.

NORTHERN IRELAND

Soldiers taking a break in the divided city of Londonderry.

Protestant and they live on Shankill Road in Belfast. Fergus's father is a policeman in the Royal Ulster Constabulary (RUC), the Northern Ireland police force. One Saturday Fergus and his parents were sitting down to lunch when they heard a huge bang. A bomb had exploded inside a crowded fish shop on Shankill Road and killed 10 people, including the young terrorist who had brought it into the shop. Fergus was told to stay inside, but he slipped out anyway. He saw his father and other policemen trying to keep the crowds away so that ambulance crews could take away the dead and injured.

When his father came home much later he was tired and angry. "Of course it was a Catholic bomb," he said, "the work of the Irish Republican Army. We'll never get peace around here." Fergus is confused too—why can't Catholics and Protestants find a way of living together?

NORTHERN IRELAND

Gerry Adams, President of Sinn Fein (Ourselves Alone), helps carry the coffin of IRA bomber Thomas Begley, aged 18, in 1993. Begley was killed while he was planting a bomb in a crowded fish shop on Shankill Road, Belfast.

(Right) A modern map showing the six counties of Northern Ireland.

Ireland has the oldest terrorism problem in Europe. People often think the conflict is simply one between Catholics and Protestants in Northern Ireland, but that does not tell the whole story. The real division is between the Unionists, who want the six provinces of Northern Ireland to stay British, and the Republicans, who want an independent republic of Ireland.

Background of the Northern Ireland problem

In the sixteenth century, the English king Henry VIII quarrelled with the Catholic Church and set himself up as the head of the Church of England. But he wanted to keep control over Ireland, which was largely Catholic, so he sent many of his noblemen to settle there. They took the best land away from the native Irish and tried to force them to become Protestant. Some of them joined the United Ireland Society, led by a man named Wolfe Tone. He led a rebellion against the English in 1798, but this was soon defeated.

NORTHERN IRELAND

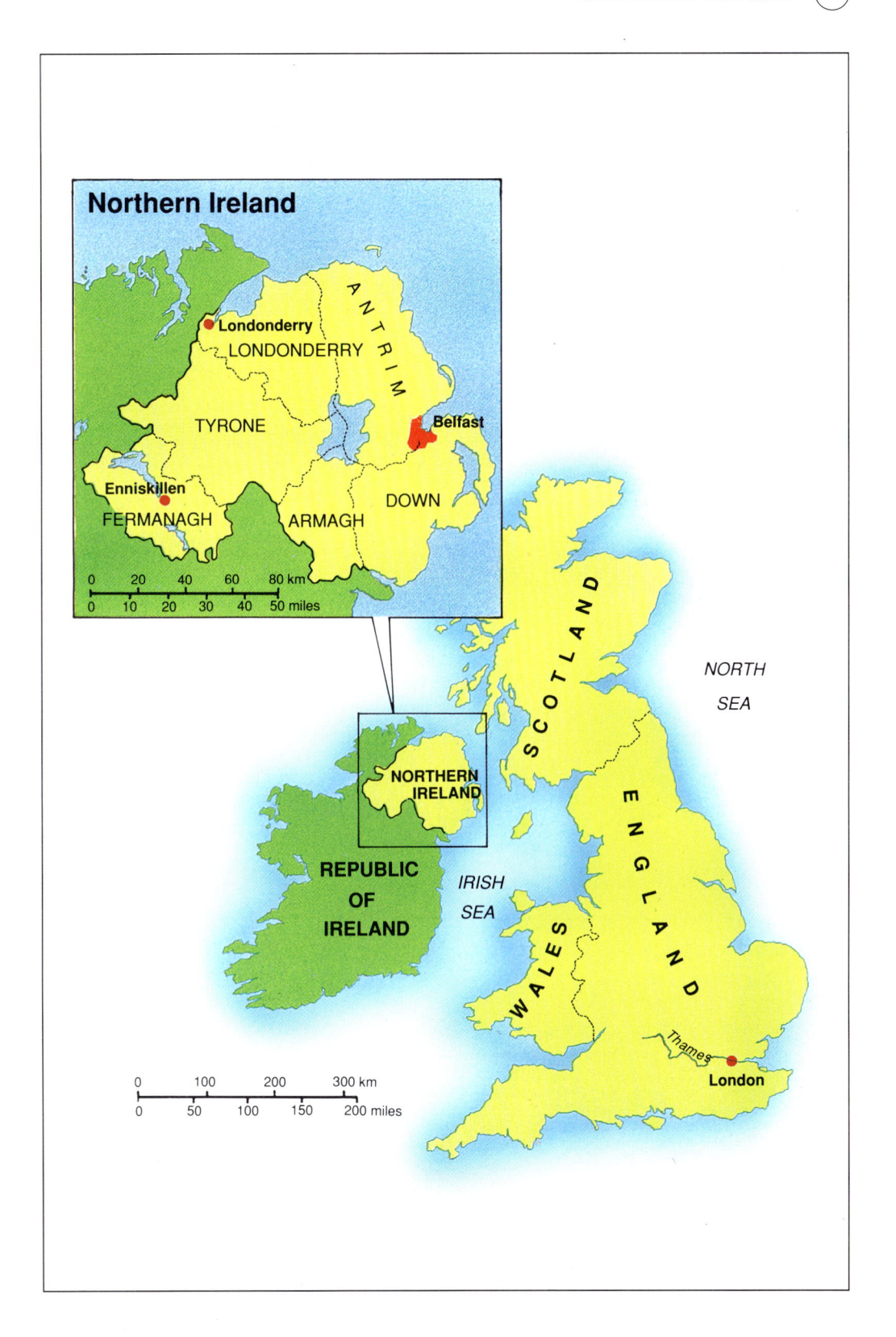

NORTHERN IRELAND

In 1801 Ireland was forced to join the United Kingdom of Great Britain. But the English were often "absentee landlords" and did not spend enough time taking care of their Irish lands. After a terrible famine in 1845, many Irish people went to live in the United States, where they founded a secret society to fight for Ireland's independence. Groups of Fenians, as they were called, came back to Europe and carried out bombing attacks against the English in Ireland and in London.

The Irish Free State
In 1916, Republicans seized control of the post office and other important buildings in Dublin, the capital of Ireland. But this "Easter Rising" was defeated, and all the leaders were executed. Finally, in 1922, after three years of civil war, part of Ireland was given independence. It was called the Irish Free State. Later it became the Republic of Ireland, or Eire. But the conflict is not over, because six counties in the north of Ireland remain British, and Ireland's constitution declares they should belong to Ireland.

In the 1960s, two-thirds of the population of Northern Ireland were Protestant and one third was Catholic. The Protestants felt themselves to be British, not Irish. The Catholics felt that they were not treated as equals by the Protestants. They felt discriminated against—

Protestant "Orangemen" celebrate the victory of King William III of Orange over Catholic forces at the Battle of Boyne in 1690. July 12, the anniversary of the battle, is still an important event in Northern Ireland.

NORTHERN IRELAND

and they were right. Although both groups were supposed to have equal rights, Protestants got better houses and better jobs than Catholics. In 1961, out of 332 senior managers of public companies, 283, or 85 percent, were Protestant and only 49 were Catholic. [9]

In 1968 a civil rights association was formed in Northern Ireland to demand equality for Catholics. Protest marches took place and some of these turned into riots. On the day of a Protestant holiday in August 1969, violence broke out in Londonderry. A battalion of British soldiers was sent in to restore order. But the rioting spread, and in Belfast seven people were killed and 750 injured. In January 1972, soldiers fired on civil rights marchers, killing 13 Catholics. The Northern Irish parliament, located in Stormont, could not control the situation, and in March the British government in London took over direct rule of Northern Ireland.

"Bloody Sunday" in Londonderry, January 30, 1972. Boys pray over a civil rights banner stained with the blood of some of the 13 victims killed by British paratroopers.

Fact File

The Enniskillen bombing

Gordon Wilson used to sell curtains and cushions in his store in Enniskillen, in the south of Ulster. One Sunday morning in November 1987 he went out with his daughter Marie, a 20-year-old student nurse. A ceremony was being held to remember all the townspeople, both Catholic and Protestant, who had been killed in the two world wars. As the crowd was gathering, a bomb hidden behind the wall of a nearby community center went off. It killed 11 people and wounded more than 60 others. The youngest person to die was Marie Wilson. Her father was holding her hands as she lay in the rubble and spoke her last words, "Daddy, I love you very much." Mr. Wilson said afterward that he forgave the killers and was praying for them. The IRA admitted planting the bomb but said it was intended for a British army patrol, not the Remembrance Day crowd.

Ever since then, Mr. Wilson has devoted his life to the cause of peace. Some people think he is a saint, while others think he is crazy. He went on living in Enniskillen but started going to Dublin two days a week. He was elected senator in the Irish parliament. He even managed to have a meeting with some members of the IRA.

This is how he described it: "I asked them to meet me, as the father of one of their victims, acknowledging that they too had had their losses. They presented me with a typed sheet of paper saying they were sorry about Enniskillen and my daughter, and repeated they were not the aggressors, but responded to British aggression. I challenged them, why, if their targets were the army and the police, had they killed eleven gentle folk in Enniskillen. It was the only time I raised my voice in anger. In Warrington, I said, you killed two little boys on a Saturday morning where there was no army or police. And they said that was a mistake. I said I am tired of hearing the IRA talking about mistakes. And really, it was then we realized we weren't getting anywhere. I drove home alone that evening and cried because I truly felt I'd let down so many people." [10]

NORTHERN IRELAND 49

Enniskillen, Northern Ireland, scene of an IRA "mistake." Of the 11 people killed, seven were elderly retirees and one was a student nurse. Seventy others were injured in the blast.

NORTHERN IRELAND

The Irish Republican Army

Between 1969 and 1993 more than three thousand people were killed as a result of the Northern Ireland conflict. About two-thirds of the murders were committed by the Irish Republican Army, one-third by Loyalist terrorists. The IRA said it would not stop the violence until all the British soldiers and representatives of the British government left Northern Ireland.

The 23-story Commercial Union Building in the City of London, destroyed by an IRA bomb in April 1992. It was the largest bomb the IRA had ever used.

The IRA is an illegal organization, but in 1994 it was thought to have about 1,500 active members. It also has a political wing called Sinn Fein, which is legal, even though it supports the IRA. Sinn Fein's president, Gerry Adams, carried the coffin at the funeral of the young Shankill Road bomber in October 1993.

The IRA terrorist campaign has three parts: attacks on British soldiers and symbols of British rule; attacks on "economic targets," that is, bombing or setting fire to factories, hotels, shopping centers, and offices; and attacks on mainland Britain. The IRA knows that the British government pays more attention when a bomb explodes in London or in other English cities than when one goes off in Northern Ireland. The IRA hopes the British people will feel that the cost in money and in human lives is simply not worth keeping Northern Ireland. Then the British government might decide to get out of Northern Ireland.

Anti-British demonstrators in the Bogside area of Londonderry are forced to retreat in a haze of tear gas.

The Unionists

The aims and targets of the Protestant terrorist groups are different. Like all Unionists, they are afraid that Britain may one day leave Northern Ireland. The Catholic population is growing faster than the Protestant one, and the Protestants think that one day the Catholics might turn around and discriminate against them. Protestants have formed terrorist groups as a reaction to the IRA and to defend against a Catholic majority, and they want to show they can do so. They have murdered members of the IRA and people who support it. They also take revenge for murders carried out by the IRA. Sometimes they kill Catholics for no reason except that they are Catholics. But both sides have accidentally killed people other than their intended targets.

NORTHERN IRELAND

A joint declaration

At the end of 1993 the British prime minister John Major and the Irish prime minister Albert Reynolds signed an important joint declaration. First, it said that Britain would not stand in the way of a united Ireland if the majority of the people of Northern Ireland wished it. Second, it said that the Irish Republic would be prepared to give up its claim to rule over the whole of Ireland if the majority voted for British rule. The people of Ireland would decide their own future.

The two leaders hoped that the joint declaration would be a starting point for new peace talks. They wanted to get all the political leaders talking around a table. There would be no peace until guns stopped firing and people stopped hating. The declaration led to a proposal from the IRA for a ceasefire in 1994. The Loyalists then also proposed a ceasefire. Peace in Ireland now depends on whether both sides will permanently lay down their weapons.

Albert Reynolds, the Irish prime minister, with British prime minister John Major. Their joint declaration was seen as an important step toward peace in Northern Ireland.

NORTHERN IRELAND

Fact File

Some major IRA terrorist actions
November 1974: Two IRA bombs in pubs in Birmingham, England, kill 21 and wound 162.
February 1978: IRA bomb in Belfast hotel kills 12.
August 1979: IRA landmines kill 18 British soldiers in Warrenpoint, Northern Ireland.
August 1979: IRA bomb in Mullaghmore Harbor, in the Irish Republic, kills Earl Mountbatten (Queen Elizabeth II's uncle) and three others.
July 20, 1982: IRA bombs kill 11 soldiers, injure 51 in Hyde Park and Park Lane, London.
October 1984: IRA bomb in Grand Hotel, Brighton, England, intended for prime minister Margaret Thatcher, kills 5 and injures 34.
August 1988: IRA car bomb, Northern Ireland, kills 8 British soldiers and injures 29.
February 1991: IRA fire mortar bombs at windows of 10 Downing Street, London, the British prime minister's residence. No one is hurt.
April 1992: IRA car bomb in the City of London kills 3 and injures 90.
March 1993: IRA bombs in shopping center in Warrington, England, kill Jonathan Ball (aged 3) and Timothy Parry (aged 12), and injure 56.

Media Watch

Shoot to kill
In 1988 three known members of the IRA were found to be in the British territory of Gibraltar, next to Spain. It was thought that they were planning a bomb attack against a regiment of British soldiers there. A unit from the Special Air Services (SAS) regiment of the British army was sent to Gibraltar. The SAS soldiers thought the three terrorists would be armed and shot them dead without trying to arrest them or even to wound them. In fact the terrorists were not armed. This policy of shooting first and asking questions later has been called a "shoot-to-kill policy."

After the killings, a car full of explosives was found. It was clear that the IRA members were indeed planning a terrorist attack. A British television movie was made about the shootings but the government tried to keep it from being shown. An inquest into the deaths was held in Gibraltar. It ruled that the terrorists had been killed lawfully. The names of the soldiers who shot the terrorists were not made public, and they sat behind a screen so they could not be seen.

WHAT CAN BE DONE ABOUT TERRORISM?

Terrorist acts can take place anywhere in the world, at any time, and without warning. Terrorists often attack important people such as political or military leaders. These people may be given bodyguards; they travel in bullet-proof cars, and they may have their homes and offices guarded. They know they are at risk simply because they are important. Even the Pope has had to travel in a special car with bullet-proof glass all around it since a terrorist shot and wounded him in 1981. But terrorist bombs go off in public places, too—in shopping centers, train stations, bus depots, airports, and on aircraft. When this happens anyone can be a victim just by being in the wrong place at the wrong time. How can the public be protected?

Pope John Paul II has used this "Popemobile" ever since the Turkish terrorist Ali Agea shot him while he was blessing the crowd in St. Peter's Square in Rome. The Pope later visited his would-be assassin in prison and forgave him.

WHAT CAN BE DONE ABOUT TERRORISM?

Security checks

It is impossible to guard a public place such as a station or airport completely, because thousands of people come and go each day. But most big airports and train and bus stations now have special police whose job is to watch for people who behave oddly and who might put down a bag or a case with a bomb in it. Often, announcements are made asking passengers to stay with their luggage at all times. All air travelers and their luggage have to pass through a kind of X-ray machine that can detect explosives or metal objects, such as guns. Airport workers wear identity badges with their photos and names on them. This makes it more difficult for terrorists to get close to luggage loading areas or to the aircraft.

Bill Clinton, campaigning for president of the United States in 1992. Presidents always have bodyguards. Several assassination attempts have been made on presidents. Some have succeeded, such as the assassination of president John F. Kennedy in 1963.

Every piece of luggage that travels by air has to be checked for weapons and explosives. Metal detectors are no longer enough, since many explosives and even some guns are now made of plastic. New methods are constantly being developed to detect the vapors that explosives give off.

Museums and art galleries often take security measures, too. Visitors may be asked to open their bags so that security guards can check for guns or bombs. Staff usually wear identity badges. Visitors to government offices or large companies are asked to give their own names and the name of the person they want to see. Security staff will check if they are expected, and then they may ask them to wear special visitors' badges. Most people do not mind this type of security check. They feel safer because they know that the checks are a deterrent—something that makes criminals think twice about committing a crime.

Laws against terrorism
Laws are another form of deterrent. These can be national laws, passed by each country, or international

WHAT CAN BE DONE ABOUT TERRORISM?

Fact File

International terrorist incidents in 1993

Type of event
Armed attack	89
Arson	8
Assault	1
Barricade/hostage	3
Bombing	138
Firebombing	80
Kidnapping	34
Non-air hijacking	1
Sabotage/vandalism	67
Skyjacking	2
Theft	4

Region
Africa	6
Asia	37
Eastern Europe	5
Latin America	97
Middle East	101
North America	1
Western Europe	180
Total	**427**

laws, called treaties or conventions, agreed upon by several countries together. There are several international laws against terrorism.

Governments pass laws against terrorists that are often more severe than laws against ordinary criminals. Terrorists can be given longer and harder prison sentences. They may be kept in solitary confinement. People suspected of terrorism are sometimes questioned for days on end without being allowed to sleep. Sometimes they are beaten or threatened. In the 1970s West German terrorists were kept in prison cells without windows and with electric lights on day and night.

In Northern Ireland there are special courts for terrorists. Instead of a judge and a jury, the court consists of one, or at most three, judges and no jury. One reason for this is to make sure that terrorists cannot threaten or terrorize jury members. But these trials are held in secret, so ordinary citizens cannot see for themselves that justice is done.

Former U.S. Secretary of State George Schulz once said, "Fighting terrorism will not be a clean or pleasant contest, but we have no choice but to play it." [11] His words could imply that if terrorists "play dirty," then so will governments. But most people agree that democratic countries have to act in a democratic way even with terrorists—that is, terrorists must not be tortured and they should have fair trials. If democracies stop obeying the law and use the same methods as the terrorists, then people might think there is no reason to choose between them.

Government action
If terrorism goes on for a long time and involves many people, the problem is not just one of law and order but of politics. Governments must decide what to do. They have several choices: do nothing; talk to terrorists and try to reach an agreement; order special force or special laws

WHAT CAN BE DONE ABOUT TERRORISM?

to be used; or refuse to have anything to do with countries that may be supporting or sponsoring terrorism. None of these four ways is "the" solution to terrorism. Sometimes governments respond too severely or not severely enough. Even if governments offer compromises, the terrorist groups may not accept them.

Fact File

A Tamil Tiger ready for action. Many nationalist terrorist groups like the Tamil Tigers earn money to pay for their weapons by trafficking drugs.

The Tamil Tigers

Sri Lanka, once called Ceylon, is an island south of India. It was ruled by the Portuguese, the Dutch, and then the British until independence in 1948. There are two main groups on the island: the Tamils, who are of the Hindu religion; and the Sinhalese, who are Buddhist. After independence the Tamils were discriminated against by the Sinhalese. A terrorist group called the Tamil Tigers was formed in the early 1970s. It wanted an independent state in the northeast of the island. Another terrorist group called JVP wanted independence for the Sinhalese.

There was fighting between the two sides and against the Sri Lankan government during the 1980s. The Tamil Tigers hijacked a bus in 1986; they picked out the Sinhalese and killed them all. In June 1987 they murdered 29 Buddhist monks. The government decided to use force against the terrorists, and the areas where the Tamils lived were attacked and bombed. Then the Indian government brought the two sides together for peace talks. The Sri Lankan government said the Tamils could rule themselves in the north and east. They promised that the Tamil and English languages would have equal status to Sinhalese. But even this did not put an end to the terrorism there. Fighting has continued among rival terrorist groups and the government forces. Five thousand people were killed in 1989 alone.

WHAT CAN BE DONE ABOUT TERRORISM?

The future

Terrorism will probably always go on somewhere in the world. There will always be people who feel anger and hatred for their governments and who are prepared to use violence against them. Some forms of terrorism may disappear. This can happen either when one side accepts the victory of the other, or when a compromise or agreement is found. Sometimes a terrorist group realizes it has no support, and then it cannot survive. This is what happened with the left-wing terrorist groups in Western Europe. But new forms of terrorism may appear. Drug traffickers in South America use terrorism; terrorist gangs have appeared in Russia and in other countries of Eastern Europe. They have carried out kidnappings and hijackings. Once, governments in these countries were so strict that people who protested were simply killed. Television and newspapers were not allowed to talk about terrorism. So, strangely enough, democracy has made space for terrorism.

Nelson Mandela was arrested in 1962 and sentenced to life imprisonment by a South African court for being the head of a terrorist organization, the African National Congress (ANC). The ANC was called a terrorist group because it used violence against the political system called apartheid (apartness). In this system only white people could vote and own land. The black majority struggled for many years against apartheid and was supported by people around the world.

Nelson Mandela was set free in 1990, after 27 years in prison. He decided to continue the struggle against apartheid, but to do so peacefully. He did not hate the white people; he wanted to live at peace with them. The ANC and the white government of President F. W. De Klerk found a compromise.

Movies about terrorism
Several movies have been made about terrorism, such as *The Day of the Jackal*, *The Taking of Pelham One Two Three*, and *The Bodyguard* with Kevin Costner (above). They were fictional stories.

Movies have also been made about real-life terrorism. These include *The Moro Kidnap*, about the kidnapping and murder of Italian politician Aldo Moro, and *In the Name of the Father*, about people wrongly sent to prison because they were suspected of being IRA terrorists. When a movie is made from true life, the people who were involved are often asked to help make the movie. Some do, but others want to forget what happened and think a movie can never tell the whole truth.

Some people say making movies about terrorism will make people want to become terrorists because what is happening looks glamorous and exciting.

WHAT CAN BE DONE ABOUT TERRORISM ?

Democratic elections were held in April 1994. For the first time, all adults could vote, whatever their color. The ANC took the most votes, and in May Nelson Mandela became president of South Africa.

For some people, Nelson Mandela was never a terrorist, but always a freedom fighter. Others say he was a terrorist, but he stopped being one when he decided to use peaceful methods. Whatever definitions political theorists devise for terrorism, someone will disagree with them. In the end, one must make up one's own mind about whether a particular form of violence is terrorism or a struggle for independence.

Democracy came to South Africa with the general election of 1994. People walked for miles, sometimes carrying elderly relatives on their backs, and waited patiently for hours in order to vote for the first time in their lives.

SOURCES OF QUOTES

1. Adriana Faranda, member of the Italian Red Brigades, in *The Heart Attacked* by Alison Jamieson. New York: Marion Boyars Publishers, 1989.
2. IRA leader in Magill, November 1981, quoted in H. H. Tucker (ed.), *Combating the Terrorists*. New York: Facts on File, 1988.
3. Mao Tse-tung, from a speech given November 6, 1938; it appears in his *Selected Works*, Vol. II (Beijing: Foreign Languages Press, 1965).
4. David Fromkin, "The Strategy of Terrorism" in *International Terrorism*, Charles W. Kegley, ed. New York: St. Martin's Press, 1990.
5. Former British prime minister Margaret Thatcher, quoted in *Invisible Armies* by Stephen Segaller. London: Sphere Books, 1987.
6. Franz Fanon, *The Wretched of the Earth*. New York: Grove Weidenfeld, 1991.
7. Eileen MacDonald, *Shoot the Women First*. New York: Random House, 1991.
8. Bruce Hoffman, *Holy Terror: The Implications of Terrorism Motivated by a Religious Imperative*. Santa Monica, CA: Rand Corporation, 1993.
9. Bishop Patrick and Mallie Eamon, *The Provisional IRA*. London: Heinemann, 1987.
10. Interview in *The Times*, London, November 5, 1993.
11. George P. Schulz, "Terrorism and the Modern World" in Walter Laqueur and Yonah Alexander (eds.) *The Terrorism Reader*. New York: NAL-Dutton, 1987.

GLOSSARY

Absentee landlords Landowners who are often away or absent from their land.
Aggressor, aggression One who attacks first, hostility.
Aryan race Does not exist as such, but used to describe white, fair-haired, fair-skinned people of northern European origin.
Buddhist A follower of the religion based on teachings of Guatama Buddha.
Civilians People who are not in the armed forces.
Cold blood (to murder in) To murder calmly and coldly without provocation.
Compromise Agreement reached after each side has given something to the other.
Declaration Formal statement.
Democratic Used to describe a society in which all adults have a right to vote for the government.
Discriminate against Treat unfairly, take sides against.
Effigy A crude figure representing a hated person.
Extremist An advocate of extreme political measures; someone whose views are dangerously strong.
Hindu Belonging to the Indian religion of Hinduism.
Humane Kind, considerate.
Islam The religious faith of Muslims, which includes belief in the prophet Muhammad.
Massacre Killing of a large number of people.
Moderate Tolerant, not extreme.
Mosque Place of worship for Muslims.
Muslim Belonging to the Islamic religion.
Oppressed Treated with cruelty or injustice.
Refugee camps Camps where people live when they have been forced to flee from their own country and have no homes to go to.

FURTHER READING

Non-fiction

Dobson, Christopher & Payne, Ronald. *The Terrorists: Their Weapons, Leaders and Tactics.* Revised edition. New York: Facts on File, 1982.

Gearty, Conor. *Terror.* Winchester, MA: Faber & Faber, 1992.

Killeen, Richard. *The Easter Rising.* Revolution! New York: Thomson Learning, 1995.

Lang, Susan S. *Extremist Groups in America.* New York: Franklin Watts, 1990.

Laqueur, Walter and Alexander, Yonah. *The Terrorism Reader.* New York: NAL-Dutton, 1987.

Lawson, Don. *America Held Hostage: From the Tehran Embassy Takeover and the Iran-Contra Affair.* Twentieth Century American History. New York: Franklin Watts, 1991.

Reische, Diana. *Arafat and the Palestine Liberation Organization.* International Affairs. New York: Franklin Watts, 1991.

Fiction

Clancy, Tom. *Patriot Games.* New York: Putnam Publishing Group, 1987.

Conrad, Joseph *The Secret Agent.* New York: Penguin, 1907, 1963.

Le Carre, John. *The Little Drummer Girl.* New York: Alfred A. Knopf, 1981.

FURTHER INFORMATION

The North Atlantic Assembly is the inter parliamentary assembly of member countries of the North Atlantic Alliance. The Sub-Commission on Terrorism publishes annual reports that are available from:

North Atlantic Assembly
International Secretariat
Place du Petit Sablon 3
1000 Brussels
Belgium

Other organizations that regularly publish studies on terrorism and political violence are:

The Rand Corporation
2100 M Street NW
Washington, DC 20037
The Rand Corporation publishes the journal *Studies in Conflict and Terrorism.*

Research Institute for the Study of Conflict and Terrorism (RISCT)
136 Baker Street
London W1M IFH
England

INDEX

Numbers in **bold** indicate subjects shown in pictures.

abortion clinic bombings 4
Abu Nidal Organization (ANO) 35
Achille Lauro hijack 15-16, **15**
Adams, Gerry 44, 51
African National Congress (ANC) 59-60
airport security 55, **56**
Algeria 19, **19**
anarchists 18, 20, 23
Angry Brigades 10
Arabs 8, 30-31, **30**
Arafat, Yasser 33, 35-36, **36**
assassination 10, 13, 18, **18**

Begin, Menachem **39**
Belfast 12, **12**, 42, 47
Black Panthers 24
Black September 34-35, **35**
Bloody Sunday 47
bodyguards 54, **55**
bomb explosions **8, 29, 44, 48-49, 50**
bombs **12**, 12-13, 54
Bosnia 26, **26**
Britain 10, 28, 29, 30, 35, 42-44, 46, 50-52

Carter, Jimmy, President **39**
Catholics 42, 43, 44, 46-47, 51
Christian Identity Movement 26-27
Clinton, Bill, President **55**
Commercial Union Building bombing **50**
Contras 29

Dawsons Field hijack 33-34
de Klerk, F.W., South African President 59
democracy 7-8, 24, 25, 29, 59
drug traffickers 58, 59

Easter Rising 46
Egypt 39-41
Enniskillen bombing 48, **48-49**
ethnic cleansing 25-27

Fanon, Franz 22
Fascism 5
Fenians 46
France 18, 22
freedom fighters 4, 60
French Resistance 7, **7**
French Revolution 18

Gadhafi, Mu'ammar al-, Colonel **28**, 28-29
Gaza Strip 30, 31, 36

Germany 5, 13, 26, 27, 28, 34-35
Gibraltar 53
Golan Heights 30, 31
Goldstein, Baruch 37
guerrillas 22, **23**, 24, **24**
Guevara, Che 22, **23**
guns 11, **13**

Hamas 37
Henry VIII, King 44
Hezbollah 38-39
hijacking 4, 10-11, **14**, 15-17, **15**, **16**, 21, **20-21**, 34, 59
Hitler, Adolf 27-28, **27**
Hong Kong Bank bomb explosion **8**
hostage taking 4, 10-11, **11**, **14**, 15-17, 21, 33-34
Hussein, King 34

Indonesia 17
Intifada 31, 33
Iranian embassy siege **6**
Irish Free State 46
Irish Republican Army (IRA) 13, **13**, 19, 28, 43, 48, 50-51, 52, 53
Islamic Brotherhood 13, 39-41
Islamic fundamentalism 37-41
Israelis 10, 15, 31, 33, 34-35, 37, 39
Italy 15, 18, 25, 26

Jews 26-28, 30-31
"just cause" 6-7, 10, 17, 19

Kach 37
Khomeini, Ayatollah 38, **38**
kidnapping 4, 10, 17, 25, 59
Koran 37

laws 56-57
Lebanon 35, 38-39
left-wing terrorism 22-25, **23**, **24**, 59
Libya 28-29
Lockerbie plane crash 29, **29**

Major, John, British prime minister 52, **52**
Mandela, Nelson, South African president 59-60
Mao Tse-tung 10, **10**, 24
martyrs 19
media 17, 18, 21, 32
Moro, Aldo, Italian prime minister 25, 59

Munich Olympics 34, **34**
Muslims 27, **27**, 37, 40

National Liberation Front (FLN) 22
Nazis 5, **27**
newspapers 10, 17, 18, 21, 59
Nicaragua 29
Northern Ireland 8, 42-43
    background of the problem 44-47
    Enniskillen bombing 48-49
    IRA terrorism 50-51, 53
    joint declaration 52
    Unionists 51

Orangemen **46**

Palestine 8, 30-37
Palestine Liberation Organization (PLO) 13, 19, 33, 34, 35, 36, 37
Pope, the 54, **54**
protesters 4
Protestants 42, 43, 44, 46-47, 51

Rabin, Yitzhak, Israeli Prime Minister 36, **36**
Rahman, Sheikh Omar Abdul 40-41
Red Army Faction 12-13, 25, 26
Red Brigades 25, **25**, 26
refugee camps 31, **35**, 36
Reign of Terror 18
religion 4, 6, 37, 42-47, 51
religious terrorism 23, 37
Republic of Ireland 46
revolutionaries 18-20, 23, 24
Reynolds, Albert, Irish Prime Minister 52, **52**
right-wing terrorism 26-27
Royal Ulster Constabulary (RUC) 43
Russia 18, 22, 59
Russian Revolution 18, **18**

Sadat, Anwar **39**, 40
security checks 55-56
Shankill Road bombing 43, **44**, 51
Shebab 31, 33
Shining Path **24**
Sinn Fein 44, 51, 52
Six Day War 31
South Africa 59-60
South Moluccan terrorists 17
Sri Lanka 58
state terrorism 18, 28-29
Symbionese Liberation Army 24

Tamil Tigers 58
television 17, 18, 21, 53, 59
Tone, Wolfe 44
torture 6
Tupamaros 22
TWA hijack **16**, **20-21**, 21

Unionists 43, 51
United Nations (UN) 31, 36
United States 24, 25-26, 29, 35, 37, 38-39, 46
Uruguay 23-24

violence 4, 6, 7

Weather Underground 24
West Bank 30, 31
Wilson, Gordon 48
World Trade Center bombing 41
World War II 7, 27

Zionists 30-31